# *In Search of* Alias Grace

*On Writing Canadian Historical Fiction*

Margaret Atwood

*Printed and bound in Canada / Imprimé et relié au Canada*

ISBN 0-7766-0449-X

*Charles R. Bronfman Lecture in Canadian Studies*

# *In Search of* Alias Grace

## *On Writing Canadian Historical Fiction*

Margaret Atwood

*Public Lecture*

*November 21, 1996*

*University of Ottawa*

University of Ottawa Press

**Université d'Ottawa**

*Conférence Charles R. Bronfman en Études canadiennes*

CETTE CONFÉRENCE DE PRESTIGE ANNUELLE SE TIENT GRÂCE À UN DON DE CHARLES R. BRONFMAN AUQUEL S'AJOUTE UNE SUBVENTION D'APPOINT DU MINISTÈRE DU PATRIMOINE CANADIEN. LE BUT DE LA CONFÉRENCE EST D'ENCOURAGER LA DIFFUSION DU SAVOIR PAR L'INVITATION DE PERSONNALITÉS QUI ONT CONTRIBUÉ DE FAÇON SIGNIFICATIVE À L'ÉTUDE DU CANADA. COMPTE TENU DU CARACTÈRE BILINGUE DE L'UNIVERSITÉ D'OTTAWA ET DE SA SITUATION AU CŒUR DE LA CAPITALE NATIONALE, LA CONFÉRENCE CHARLES R. BRONFMAN SE FAIT SUR UNE BASE D'ALTERNANCE DANS L'UNE OU L'AUTRE DES LANGUES OFFICIELLES DU PAYS.

LA PUBLICATION DE LA CONFÉRENCE A ÉTÉ RÉALISÉE GRÂCE À UNE SUBVENTION DU PROJET REFLETS DU PATRIMOINE DE LA FONDATION CRB HÉRITAGE CANADA.

**University of Ottawa**

*Charles R. Bronfman Lecture in Canadian Studies*

THIS DISTINGUISHED YEARLY LECTURE IS MADE POSSIBLE THANKS TO A DONATION FROM CHARLES R. BRONFMAN AND TO A GRANT FROM THE CANADIAN STUDIES PROGRAM OF THE DEPARTMENT OF CANADIAN HERITAGE. THE LECTURE SEEKS TO PROMOTE SCHOLARSHIP BY INVITING PERSONALITIES WHO HAVE MADE A SIGNIFICANT CONTRIBUTION TO THE STUDY OF CANADA. GIVEN THE BILINGUAL CHARACTER OF THE UNIVERSITY OF OTTAWA AND ITS LOCATION IN THE HEART OF THE NATION'S CAPITAL, THE CHARLES R. BRONFMAN LECTURE IS GIVEN IN ONE OR THE OTHER OF CANADA'S OFFICIAL LANGUAGES, ON AN ALTERNATING BASIS.

PUBLICATION OF THE LECTURE HAS BEEN MADE POSSIBLE THROUGH A GRANT FROM THE CRB FOUNDATION HERITAGE PROJECT.

## *Introduction*

Margaret Atwood was born in Ottawa, Ontario, in 1939. During her childhood she spent many summers in the bush country of northern Ontario and Quebec. Upon graduation from the University of Toronto in 1961, she took her master's degree from Radcliffe College the following year and went on to pursue doctoral studies at Harvard University.

Novelist and poet, critic and editor, Atwood is one of the most prolific and important writers of contemporary literature. Equally acclaimed as a writer of both fiction and poetry, she devotes much of her creative energy to giving literary shape to the aspirations, fears, and foibles of her society. Her many honours include the Governor General's Award for Poetry, the Governor General's Award for Fiction, the *Los Angeles Times* Fiction Award, the Giller Prize for Fiction, and several honorary degrees.

Her ninth novel, *Alias Grace*, was published in the fall of 1996.

# *In Search of* Alias Grace

## *On Writing Canadian Historical Fiction*

Margaret Atwood

*Charles R. Bronfman Lecture in Canadian Studies*

*November 21, 1996*

It is a great honour, and also a great pleasure, to be delivering the third annual Bronfman Lecture at the University of Ottawa—that is, it is a great pleasure for me. I hope it will be a pleasure for you as well, but I must put you on notice that you have invited a writer of fiction to speak to you, and these are a suspicious bunch of people. Consider what they do all day: they concoct plausible whoppers, which they hope they can induce the public to swallow whole.

In a town of politicians, this may seem like a respectable enough way of earning your living. But fiction writers do not come with the usual props and backups designed to add verisimilitude to an otherwise bald and unconvincing tale, that is, the graphs, the studies, the statistics, the blue and red books, the Royal Commissions and omissions, and so forth. Fiction writers do not pretend to be specialists or experts at anything except what Dylan Thomas termed their craft and sullen art. About all they really know anything about is the writing of their latest book, and they're usually not even sure how they managed that, having done it in a sort of stupor; and if they do know, they aren't about to tell, any more than a magician will hasten to reveal exactly how he made the pigeon come out of your ear.

But here I am, advertised as a person who will communicate to you something or other having to do with Canadian Studies; and having been brought up by the Girl Guides, where we were taught that the boxes of cookies we were peddling had to contain actual cookies, however eccentric in texture and taste, I always try—unlike some of more political avocation—to live up to the claims on the package.

So what I am going to talk about this evening does have to do with Canadian Studies—more particularly the Canadian novel, and even more particularly, the Canadian historical novel. I will address the nature of this genre insofar as it has to do with the mysteries of time and memory; I will meditate on why so many of this kind of novel have been written lately by English-speaking Canadian authors; and after that I will talk a little about my own recent attempt to write such a novel. At the end I will try to add on some sort of meaning-of-it-all nugget or philosophical summation, as such a thing is implicitly called for in the list of ingredients on the cookie box.

Fiction is where individual memory and experience and collective memory and experience come together, in greater or lesser proportions. The closer the fiction is to us as readers, the more we recognize and claim it as individual rather than collective. Margaret Laurence used to say that her English readers thought *The Stone Angel* was about old age, the Americans thought it was about some old woman they knew, and the Canadians thought it was about their grandmothers.

Each character in fiction has an individual life, replete with personal detail—the eating of meals, the flossing of teeth, the making of love, the birthing of children, the attending of funerals, and so forth—but each also exists within a context, a fictional world comprised of geology, weather, economic forces, social classes, cultural references, and wars and plagues and such big public events; you'll note that, being Canadian, I put the geology first. This fictional world so lovingly delineated by the writer may bear a more obvious or a less obvious relation to the world we actually live in, but bearing no relation to it at all is not an option. We have to write out of who and where and when we are, whether we like it or not, and disguise it how we may. As Robertson Davies has remarked, "we all belong to our own time, and there is nothing whatever that we can do to escape from it. Whatever we write will be contemporary, even if we attempt a novel set in a past age."[1] We cannot help but be modern, just as the Victorian writers—whenever they set their books—could not help but be Victorian. Like all beings alive on Middle Earth, we are trapped by time and circumstance.

What I've said about fictional characters is, of course, also true of every real human being. For example, here I am,

1. Robertson Davies, "Fiction of the Future," *The Merry Heart: Selections 1980–1995* (Toronto: McClelland and Stewart, 1996), p. 358.

giving this Bronfman Lecture in Ottawa. By what twists of coincidence or fate—how novelistic these terms sound, but also how faithful to real experience they are—do I find myself back here in my city of origin?

For it was in Ottawa that I was born, fifty-seven years, three days, and several hours ago. The place was the Ottawa General Hospital; the date, November 18, 1939. About the exact hour, my mother—to the despair of many astrologers since—is a little vague, that being a period when women were routinely conked out with ether. I do know that I was born after the end of the Grey Cup football game. The doctors thanked my mother for waiting; they had all been following the game on the radio. In those days most doctors were men, which may explain their sportive attitude.

"In those days"—there I am, you see, being born in *those* days, which are not the same as *these* days; no ether now, and many a woman doctor. As for Ottawa, I would not have been there at all if it had not been for the Great Depression: my parents were economic refugees from Nova Scotia—here is your economic force—from which they were then cut off by the Second World War—here is your big public event.

We lived—here is your personal detail—in a long, dark, railroad-car-shaped second-story apartment on Patterson Avenue, near the Rideau Canal—here is your geology, more or less—an apartment in which my mother once caused a flood by rinsing the diapers in the toilet, where they got stuck—in *those* days there were no disposable diapers, and not even any diaper services. In *those* days, as I'm sure some of you believe you remember, there was much more snow—here is your weather—and it was much whiter and more beautiful than any snow they ever come up with nowadays. As a child I helped to build snow forts that were much bigger than the Parliament Buildings, and even more labyrinthine—here is your cultural reference. I remember this very clearly, so it must be true, and here is your individual memory.

What is my point? It is out of such individual particulars that fiction is constructed; and so is autobiography, including the kind of autobiography we are each always writing, but have not yet got around to writing down; and so, too, is history. History may intend to provide us with grand patterns and overall schemes, but without its brick-by-brick, life-by-life, day-by-day foundations it would collapse.

Whoever tells you that history is not about individuals, only about large trends and movements, is lying. The shot heard round the world was fired on a certain date, under certain weather conditions, out of a certain rather inefficient type of gun. After the Rebellion of 1837, William Lyon Mackenzie escaped to the United States dressed in women's clothing; I know the year, so I can guess the style of his outfit. When I lived in the rural Ontario countryside north of Toronto, a local man said, "There's the barn where we hid the women and children, that time the Fenians invaded." An individual barn; individual women and children. The man who told me about the barn was born some sixty years after the Fenian attack, but he said *we*, not *they*: he was remembering as a personal experience an event at which he had not been present in the flesh, and I believe we have all done that. It is at such points that memory, history, and story all intersect; it would take only one step more to bring all of them into the realm of fiction.

We live in a period in which memory of all kinds, including the sort of larger memory we call history, is being called into question. For history as for the individual, forgetting can be just as convenient as remembering, and remembering what was once forgotten can be distinctly uncomfortable. As a rule, we tend to remember the awful things done to us, and to forget the awful things we did. The Blitz is still remembered; the fire-bombing of Dresden—well, not so much, or not by us. To challenge an accepted version of history—what we've decided it's proper to remember—by dredging up things that society has decided are better forgotten, can cause cries of anguish and outrage, as the makers of a recent documentary about the Second World War could testify. Remembrance Day, like Mother's Day, is a highly ritualized occasion; for instance, we are not allowed, on Mother's Day, to commemorate *bad* mothers, and even to acknowledge that such persons exist would be considered—on that date—to be in shoddy taste.

Here is the conundrum, for history and individual memory alike, and therefore for fiction also: how do we know we know what we think we know? And if we find that, after all, we do not know what it is that we once thought we knew, how do we know we are who we think we are, or thought we were yesterday, or thought we were—for instance—a hundred years ago? These are the questions one asks oneself, at my age, whenever one says "Whatever happened to old what's-his-name"; they are also the questions that arise in connection with Canadian history, or indeed with any other kind of history. They are also the questions that arise in any contemplation of what used to be called "character"; they are thus central to any conception of the novel.

The novel concerns itself, above all, with time. Any plot is a *this* followed by a *that*; there must be change in a novel, and change can only take place over time, and this change can only have significance if either the character in the book—or, at the very least, the reader—can remember what came before. As Henry James's biographer Leon Edel has said, if there's a clock in it, you know it's a novel.

Thus there can be no history, and no novel either, without memory of some sort; but when it comes right down to it, how reliable is memory itself—our individual memory, or our collective memory as a society? Once, memory was a given. You could lose it and you could recover it, but the thing lost and then recovered was as solid and all-of-a-piece, was as much a *thing*, as a gold coin. "Now it all comes back to me," or some version of it, was a staple of the recovering-from-amnesia scenes in Victorian melodramas—indeed, even so late as the recovering-from-amnesia scene in Graham Greene's *The Ministry of Fear*; and there was an *it*, there was an *all*. If the seventeenth century revolved around faith—that is, what you believed—and the eighteenth around knowledge—that is, what you could prove—the nineteenth could be said to have revolved around memory. You cannot have Tennyson's, "Tears, idle tears ... O Death in Life, the days that are no more," unless you can remember those days that used to be, and are no more. Nostalgia for what once was, guilt for what you once did, revenge for what someone else once did to you, regret for what you once might have done, but did not do—how central they all are to the previous century, and how dependent each one of them is on the idea of memory itself. Without memory, and the belief that it can be recovered whole, like treasure fished out of a swamp, Proust's famous *madeleine* is reduced to a casual snack. The nineteenth-century novel would be unimaginable without a belief in the integrity of memory, for what is the self without a more or less continuous memory of itself, and what is the novel without the self? Or so they would have argued back then.

As for the twentieth century, at least in Europe, it has been on the whole more interested in forgetting—forgetting as an organic process, and sometimes as a willed act. Dali's famous painting, "The Persistence of Memory," features a melting clock and a parade of destructive ants; Beckett's famous play *Krapp's Last Tape* is relentless in its depiction of how we erase and rewrite ourselves over time; Milan Kundera's novel, *The Book of Laughter and Forgetting*, has a touchstone twentieth-century title; the horrifying film *Night and Fog* is only one of many twentieth-century statements about how we industriously and systematically obliterate history to suit our own vile purposes; and in Orwell's *1984*, the place where documents are sent to be destroyed is called, ironically, the Memory Hole. The twentieth century's most prominent theories of the psyche—those that evolved from Freud—taught us that we were not so much the sum of what we could remember, as the sum of what we had forgotten.[2] We were controlled by the Unconscious, where unsavoury repressed memories were stored in our heads like rotten apples in a barrel, festering away but

2. See, for instance, Ian Hacking, *Rewriting the Soul* (Princeton: Princeton University Press, 1995).

essentially unknowable, except for the suspicious smell. Furthermore, twentieth-century European art as a whole gradually lost faith in the reliability of time itself. No longer an evenly flowing river, it became a collage of freeze-frames, jumbled fragments, and jump-cuts.[3]

The hero of Spanish writer Javier Marias's 1989 novel *All Souls* represents a host of twentieth-century European spiritual relatives when he says, "I must speak of myself and of my time in the city of Oxford, even though the person speaking is not the same person who was there. He seems to be, but he is not. If I call myself 'I', or use a name which has accompanied me since birth and by which some will remember me ... it is simply because I prefer to speak in the first person and not because I believe that the faculty of memory alone is any guarantee that a person remains the same in different times and different places. The person recounting here and now what he saw and what happened to him then is not the same person who saw those things and

3. See, for instance, Paul Fussell, *The Great War and Modern Memory* (New York and London: Oxford University Press, 1975).

to whom those things happened; neither is he a prolongation of that person, his shadow, his heir or his usurper."[4]

End of quotation. Fine and dandy, we say, with our streetwise postmodern consciousness. Problems do arise, however. If the I of now has nothing to do with the I of then, where did the I of now come from? Nothing is made from nothing, or so we used to believe. And, to get back to Canadian Studies, why is it that it is now—within the last fifteen or twenty years, and so near the end of the fragmenting and memory-denying twentieth century—that the Canadian historical novel has become so popular with writers and readers alike?

But what exactly do we mean by "historical novel"? All novels are in a sense "historical" novels; they can't help it, insofar as they have to, they *must*, make reference to a time that is not the time in which the reader is reading the book. But there is the past tense—yesterday and yesterday and yesterday, full of tooth-flossing and putting the antifreeze

4. Javier Marias, *All Souls*, translated by Margaret Jull Costa (London: The Harvill Press, 1995), p. 3.

into the car, a yesterday not so long ago—and then there is The Past, capital T and P.

Charles Dickens's Scrooge timorously asks the Ghost of Christmas Past whether the past they are about to visit is "long past," and is told, "No—your past." For a considerable period it was only "your past"—the personal past of the writer, and, by extension, that of the reader—that was at issue in the Canadian novel. I do not recall any serious writer in the sixties writing what we think of as historical romances proper, that is, the full-dress petticoat-and-farthingale kind, which were associated with subjects like Mary Queen of Scots. Perhaps it was thought that Canada lacked the appropriate clothing for such works; perhaps the genre itself was regarded as a form of trash writing, like bodice-rippers—which, like any other genre, it either is or it isn't, depending on how it's done.

Once, we as a society were not so squeamish. Major Richardson's hugely popular nineteenth-century novel *Wacousta* was, among other things, a historical novel along the lines of Sir Walter Scott, granddaddy of the form, and James Fenimore Cooper, his even more prolix descendant. These were nineteenth-century novelists, and the nineteenth century loved the historical novel. *Vanity Fair*, *Middlemarch*, *A Tale of Two Cities*, *Ivanhoe*, *Treasure Island*—all are historical novels of one kind or another, and these are only a few. Perhaps the question to be asked is not why Canadians are writing historical novels now, but why we did not do it before.

In any case, by the 1960s it was as if we had forgotten that on this continent, and especially north of the 49th parallel, there was ever a bodice to be ripped or a weak-minded lady to be rendered hysterical by the experience. We were instead taken up by the momentous discovery that we ourselves actually existed, in what was then the here and now, and we were busily exploring the implications of that.

Our generation of English-speaking Canadians—those of us who were children in the forties and adolescents in the fifties—grew up with the illusion that there was not then and never had been a Canadian literature. I say "illusion," because there had, in fact, been one; it is just that we were not told about it. The collapse of old-style English colonial imperialism had abolished the old-style school reader—the kind that used to contain excerpts from English literature, mingled with bits from our native singers and songstresses, usually so termed. Thus you could go through twelve years of schooling, back then, and come out with the impression that there had only ever been one Canadian writer, and that was Stephen Leacock.

The fifties came right after the forties and the thirties; and the double whammy of the Depression followed by the War had wiped out what in the teens and twenties had been a burgeoning indigenous publishing industry, complete with bestsellers. (Remember Mazo de la Roche? We didn't. We were told nothing about her.) Add to that the weight of the paperback book industry—completely controlled, back then, from the United States—and the advent of television, most of which came from south of the border, and you get the picture. There was radio, of course. There was the Canadian Broadcasting Corporation. There were Simon and Schuster and Our Pet, Juliette. But it wasn't much of a counterbalance.

When we hit university in the late fifties and encountered intellectual magazines, we found ourselves being fed large doses of anxiety and contempt, brewed by our very own pundits and even by some of our very own poets and fiction writers, concerning our own inauthenticity, our feebleness from the cultural point of view, our lack of a real literature, and the absence of anything you could dignify by the name of history—by which was meant interesting and copious bloodshed on our own turf. In Quebec, people were more certain of their own existence, and especially of their own persistence, although they had lots of Parisian-oriented voices to tell them how substandard they were. "In Angloland," Earle Birney's famous poem that concludes, "It's only by the lack of ghosts we're haunted," sums up the prevailing attitude of the time.

We young writers charged ahead anyway. We thought we were pretty daring to be setting our poems and stories in Toronto and Vancouver and Montreal, and even Ottawa, rather than in London or Paris or New York. We were, however, relentlessly contemporary: history, for us, either did not exist, or it had happened elsewhere, or if ours it was boring.

This is often the attitude among the young, but it was especially true of us, because of the way we had encountered our own history. Quebec has always had its own version of history, with heroes and villains, and struggle, and heartbreak, and God; God was a main feature until recently. But those of us in English Canada who went to high school when I did were not dosed with any such strong medicine. Instead we were handed a particularly anemic view of our past, insofar as we were given one at all. For others on more troubled shores were the epic battles, the heroes, the stirring speeches, the do-or-die last stands, the freezing to death during the retreat from Moscow. For us the statistics on wheat and the soothing assurances that all was well in the land of the cow and potato, not to mention—although they were mentioned—the vein of metallic ore and the stack of lumber. We looked at these things, and saw that they were good, if tedious, but we did not really examine how they had been obtained or who was profiting by them, or who did the actual work, or how much they got paid for it. Nor was much said about who inhabited this space before white Europeans arrived, bearing gifts of firearms and smallpox, because weren't we nice people? You bet we were, and nice people do not dwell on morbid subjects. I myself would have been much more interested in Canadian history if I had known that our dull Prime Minister, Mackenzie King, had believed that the spirit of his mother was inhabiting his dog, which he always consulted on public policy—it explains so much—but nobody knew about such things back then.

The main idea behind the way we were taught Canadian history seemed to be reassurance: as a country, we'd had our little differences, and a few embarrassing moments—the Rebellion of 1837, the hanging of Louis Riel, and so forth—but these had just been unseemly burps in one long gentle after-dinner nap. We were always being told that Canada had come of age. This was even a textbook title: *Canada Comes of Age*. I am not sure what it was supposed to mean—that we could vote and drink and shave and fornicate, perhaps; or that we had come into our inheritance, and could now manage our own affairs.

Our inheritance. Ah yes—the mysterious sealed box handed over by the family solicitor when young master attains his majority. But what was inside it? Many things we were not told about in school, and this is where the interest in historical writing comes in. For it's the very things that are *not* mentioned that inspire the most curiosity in us. *Why* are they not mentioned? The lure of the Canadian past, for the writers of my generation, has been partly the lure of the unmentionable—the mysterious, the buried, the forgotten, the discarded, the taboo.

This digging up of buried things began perhaps in poetry; for instance, E.J. Pratt's narrative poems on subjects like the sinking of the *Titanic* and the life of the French Jesuit missionary Brébeuf. Pratt was followed by certain younger writers; I think of Gwendolyn MacEwen's mid-sixties verse play *Terror and Erebus* about the failure of the Franklin expedition. I blush to mention Margaret Atwood's *The Journals of Susanna Moodie* of 1970, but since I'll need to mention it later on, I'll get the blushing over with now. Other poets—D.G. Jones and Al Purdy in particular, but there were more—used historic events as subjects for individual poems. James Reaney was a pioneer in the use of local history—he was writing the Donnelly trilogy in the late sixties, although the plays were not produced until later. There were other plays in the 1970s, too—Rick Salutin's *1837: The Farmers' Revolt*, about the Upper Canada Rebellion, springs to mind.

Then came the novels. These were not historical romances of the bodice-ripping kind; instead they were what we should probably term "novels set in the historic past," to distinguish them from the kind of thing you find in drugstores that have cloaks and raised silver scrollwork titles on them. When is the past old enough to be considered historic? Well, roughly, I suppose you could say it's anything before the time at which the novel-writer came to consciousness. That seems fair enough.

In the novel, then, we had Anne Hébert's excellent *Kamouraska* as early as 1970. It was written in French, but it was translated, and many English-speaking writers read it. As far back as Margaret Laurence's *The Diviners* in 1974 and Marian Engel's *Bear* in 1976, figures from the Canadian past were used as a point of reference for the Canadian present—Catharine Parr Traill by Laurence, an obscure and probably invented nineteenth-century English emigrant by Engel. Rudy Wiebe's *The Temptations of Big Bear* in 1973 and *The Scorched-Wood People* in 1977 are usually thought of as being enclosed by the parentheses *Native Peoples*, but they are, of course, set entirely in the past. Then there is Timothy Findley's *The Wars* in 1977.

In the eighties and nineties, the trend intensified. Graeme Gibson's *Perpetual Motion* was published in 1982. After that the names are legion. Robertson Davies's *Murther and Walking Spirits* is a historical novel. So—using my definition of historic—are Michael Ondaatje's *In the Skin of a*

*Lion* and *The English Patient*, and Brian Moore's *Black Robe*. So are Alice Munro's two stories "Meneseteung" and "A Wilderness Station." So are George Bowering's *Burning Water* and Daphne Marlatt's *Ana Historic*, and Jane Urquhart's *The Whirlpool* and *Away*; so is Carol Shields's *The Stone Diaries*; so is Timothy Findley's *The Piano Man's Daughter*. In this year alone, we have Gail Anderson-Dargatz's *The Cure for Death by Lightning*, Findley's *You Went Away*, Katherine Govier's *Angel Walk*, Ann-Marie MacDonald's *Fall on Your Knees*, Anne Michaels's *Fugitive Pieces*, and Guy Vanderhaeghe's *The Englishman's Boy*.

All of these are set in the past—Dickens's *long* past—but not all use the past for the same purposes. Of course not. Their authors are individuals, and each novel has its own preoccupations. Some attempt to give more or less faithful accounts of actual events, in answer perhaps to such questions as "Where did we come from and how did we get here?" Some attempt restitution of a sort, or at least an acknowledgment of past wrongs—I would put the Rudy Wiebe novels and Guy Vanderhaeghe's book in this category, dealing as they do with the deplorable North

American record on the treatment of Native Peoples. Others, such as Graeme Gibson's, look at what we have killed and destroyed in our obsessive search for the pot of gold. Others delve into class structure and political struggles—Ondaatje's *In the Skin of a Lion*, for instance. Yet others unearth a past as it was lived by women under conditions a good deal more stringent than our own; yet others use the past as background to family sagas—tales of betrayal and tragedy and even madness. "The past is a foreign country," begins the English novel *The Go-Between*; "they do things differently there."[5] Yes, they do, and these books point that out; but they also do quite a few things the same, and these books point that out as well.

Why, then, has there been such a spate of historical novels in the past twenty years, and especially in the past decade? Earlier, I gave some possible reasons as to why this trend did not occur earlier. But why is it occurring now?

Some might say that we are more confident about ourselves—that we are now allowed to find ourselves more

5. L.P. Hartley, *The Go-Between* (London: Hamish Hamilton, 1953), p. 9.

interesting than we once did; and I think they would be right. In this, we are part of a worldwide movement that has found writers and readers, especially in ex-colonies, turning back towards their own roots, while not rejecting developments in the imperial centres. London and Paris are still wonderful places, but they are no longer seen as the only homes of the good, the true, and the beautiful, as well as of those more typical twentieth-century tastes, the bad, the false, and the ugly. You want squalor, lies, and corruption? Hell, we've got 'em home-grown, and not only that, we always have had, and there's where the past comes in.

Some might say that, on the other hand, the past is safer; that at a time when our country feels very much under threat—the threat of splitting apart, and the threat of having its established institutions and its social fabric and its sense of itself literally torn to pieces—it feels comforting to escape backwards, to a time when these things were not the problems. With the past, at least we know what happened: while visiting there, we suffer from no uncertainties about the future, or at least the part of it that comes in between them and us; we've read about it. The *Titanic* may be sinking, but we're not on it. Watching it subside, we're diverted for a short time from the leaking lifeboat we're actually in right now.

Of course the past was not really safer. As a local museum custodian once commented, "Nostalgia is the past without the pain," and for those living in it, the past was their present, and just as painful as our present is to us—and perhaps more so, considering the incurable diseases and the absence of anesthesia, central heating, and indoor plumbing back then, to mention a few of the drawbacks. Those who long for a return to the supposed values of the nineteenth century should turn away from the frilly-pillow magazines devoted to that era and take a good hard look at what was really going on. So although cosiness may be an attraction, it is also an illusion; and not many of the Canadian historical novels I have mentioned depict the past as a very soothing place.

There is also the lure of time travel, which appeals to the little cultural anthropologist in each one of us. It's such fun to snoop, as it were; or to peek in the windows. What did they eat, back then? What did they wear, how did they wash their clothes, or treat their sick, or bury their dead? What did they think about? What lies did they tell, and why? Who were they really? The questions, once they begin, are endless. It's like questioning your dead great-grandparents—does any of what they did or thought live on in us.

I think there is another reason for the appeal, and it has to do with the age we are now. Nothing is more boring to a fifteen-year-old than Aunt Agatha's ramblings about the family tree; but often, nothing is more intriguing to a fifty-year-old. It is not the individual authors who are now fifty—some of them are a good deal younger than that. I think it is the culture.

I once took a graduate course entitled "The Literature of the American Revolution," which began with the professor saying that there actually *was* no literature of the American Revolution, because everyone was too busy revolting during that period to write any, and so we were going to study the literature just before it and the literature just after it. What came after it was a lot of hand-wringing and soul-searching on the part of the American artistic community, such as it was. Now that we've had the Revolution, they fretted, where is the great American genius that ought to burst forth? What should the wondrous novel or poem or painting be like in order to be truly American? Why can't we have an

American fashion industry? And so on. When *Moby Dick* and Walt Whitman finally did appear, most right-thinking people wiped their feet on them; but such is life.

It was out of this questioning and assessing climate, however—where did we come from, how did we get from there to here, where are we going, who are we now—that Nathaniel Hawthorne wrote *The Scarlet Letter*, a historical novel set in seventeenth-century New England. The eighteenth century had mostly been embarrassed by the Puritans, and especially by their crazed zeal during the Salem witchcraft trials, and had tried to forget about them; but Hawthorne dug them up again, and took a long hard look at them. *The Scarlet Letter* is not, of course, seventeenth-century in any way the Puritans would have recognized; in good nineteenth-century style, it is far too admiring and respectful of that adulterous baggage, Hester Prynne. Instead it is a novel that uses a seventeenth-century New England colonial setting for the purposes of a newly forged nineteenth-century American Republic. And I think that's part of the interest for writers and readers of Canadian historical fiction, now: by taking a long hard look backwards, we place ourselves.

Having more or less delivered two of the three main things I promised you, I will now turn to the third, that is, my own attempt to write a piece of fiction set in the past. I did not plan to do it, but I somehow ended up doing it anyway, which is how my novels generally occur. Nor was I conscious of any of the motives I have just outlined. I think novelists begin with hints and images and scenes and voices rather than with theories and grand schemes. Individual characters interacting with, and acted upon by, the world that surrounds them are what interests the novel; the details, not the large pattern, although a large pattern does then emerge.

The book in question is *Alias Grace*, and here is how it came about. In the sixties, for reasons that cannot be rationally explained, I found myself writing a sequence of poems called *The Journals of Susanna Moodie*, which was about an English emigrant who came to what is now Ontario in the 1830s, and had a truly awful time in a swamp north of Peterborough, and wrote about her experiences in a book called *Roughing It in the Bush*, which warned English gentlefolk not to do the same. Canada, in her opinion, was a land suited only to horny-handed peasants, otherwise known as honest sons of toil. After she escaped from the woods, she wrote *Life in the Clearings versus the Bush*, which contains her version of the Grace Marks story.

Susanna Moodie describes her meeting with Grace in the Kingston Penitentiary in 1851; she then retells the double murder in which Grace was involved. The motive, according to Moodie, was Grace's passion for her employer, the gentleman Thomas Kinnear, and her demented jealousy of Nancy Montgomery, Kinnear's housekeeper and mistress. Moodie portrays Grace as the driving engine of the affair—a scowling, sullen teenage temptress—with the co-murderer, the manservant James McDermott, shown as a mere dupe, driven on by his own lust for Grace, as well as by her taunts and blandishments.

Thomas Kinnear and Nancy Montgomery ended up dead in the cellar, and Grace and McDermott made it across Lake Ontario to the States with a wagonful of stolen goods. They were caught and brought back, and tried for the murder of Thomas Kinnear; the murder of Nancy was never tried, as both were convicted and condemned to death. McDermott was hanged. Grace was sentenced as an accessory, but as a result of petitions by her well-wishers, and in consideration of her feebler sex and extreme youth—she was barely sixteen—her sentence was commuted to life.

Moodie saw Grace again, this time in the violent ward of the newly built Lunatic Asylum in Toronto. And there her account ends, with a pious hope that perhaps the poor girl was deranged all along, which would explain her shocking behaviour and also afford her forgiveness in the afterlife. That was the first version of the story I came across, and being young, and still believing that "non-fiction" meant "true," I did not question it.

Time passed. Then, in the seventies, I was asked by CBC producer George Jonas to write a script for television. My script was about Grace Marks, using Moodie's version, which was already highly dramatic in form. In it, Grace is brooding and obsessive, and McDermott is putty in her hands. I did leave out Moodie's detail about Grace and McDermott cutting Nancy up into four pieces before hiding her under a washtub. I thought it would be hard to film, and anyway why would they have bothered?

I then received an invitation to turn my television script into a theatre piece. I did give this a try. I hoped to use a multilevelled stage so that the main floor, the upstairs, and the cellar could all be seen at once. I wanted to open the play in the Penitentiary and close it in the Lunatic Asylum, and I had some idea of having the spirit of Susanna Moodie flown in on wires, in a black silk dress, like a cross between Peter Pan and a bat; but it was all too much for me, and I gave it up, and then forgot about it.

More time passed. Soon enough it was the early 1990s, and I was on a book tour, and sitting in a hotel room in Zurich. A scene came to me vividly, in the way that scenes often do. I wrote it down on a piece of hotel writing paper, lacking any other kind; it was much the same as the opening scene of the book as it now exists. I recognized the locale: it was the cellar of the Kinnear house, and the female figure in it was Grace Marks. Not immediately, but after a while, I continued with the novel. This time, however, I did what neither Moodie nor I had done before: I went back to the past.

The past is made of paper; sometimes, now, it's made of microfilm and CD-ROMs, but ultimately they too are made of paper. Sometimes there's a building or a picture or a grave, but mostly it's paper. Paper must be taken care of; archivists and librarians are the guardian angels of paper;

without them there would be a lot less of the past than there is, and I and many other writers owe them a huge debt of thanks.

What is on the paper? The same things that are on paper now. Records, documents, newspaper stories, eyewitness reports, gossip and rumour and opinion and contradiction. There is—as I increasingly came to discover—no more reason to trust something written down on paper then than there is now. After all, the writers-down were human beings, and are subject to error, intentional or not, and to the very human desire to magnify a scandal, and to their own biases. I was often deeply frustrated as well, not by what those past recorders had written down, but by what they had left out. History is more than willing to tell you who won the Battle of Trafalgar and which world leader signed this or that treaty, but it is frequently reluctant about the now-obscure details of daily life. Nobody wrote these things down, because everybody knew them, and considered them too mundane and unimportant to record. Thus I found myself wrestling not only with who said what about Grace, but also with how to clean a chamber pot, what footgear would have been worn in winter, the origins of quilt-pattern names, and how to store parsnips. If you are after the truth, the whole and detailed truth, and nothing but the truth, you're going to have a thin time of it if you trust to paper; but with the past, it's almost all you've got.

Susanna Moodie said at the outset of her account that she was writing the Grace Marks's story from memory, and as it turns out, her memory was no better than most. She got the location wrong, and the names of some of the participants, just for starters. Not only that, the story was much more problematic, although less neatly dramatic, than the one Moodie had told. For one thing, the witnesses—even the eye-witnesses, even at the trial itself—could often not agree; but then, how is this different from most trials? For instance, one says the Kinnear house was left in great disarray by the criminals, another says it was tidy and it was not realized at first that anything had been taken. Confronted with such discrepancies, I tried to deduce which account was the most plausible.

Then there was the matter of the central figure, about whom opinion was very divided indeed. All commentators agreed that Grace was uncommonly good-looking, but they could not agree on her height or the colour of her hair. Some said Grace was jealous of Nancy, others that Nancy was, on the contrary, jealous of Grace. Some viewed Grace as a cunning female demon, others considered her a simple-minded and terrorized victim, who had run away with McDermott only out of fear for her own life.

I discovered as I read that the newspapers of the time had their own political agendas. Canada West was still reeling from the effects of the Rebellion of 1837, and this influenced both Grace's life before the murders and her treatment at the hands of the press. A large percentage of the population—some say up to a third—left the country after the Rebellion; the poorer and more radical third, we may assume, which may account for the Tory flavour of those who remained. The exodus meant a shortage of servants, which in turn meant that Grace could change jobs more frequently than her counterparts in England could. In 1843—the year of the murder—editorials were still being written about the badness or worthiness of William Lyon Mackenzie, and as a rule, the Tory newspapers that vilified him also vilified Grace—she had, after all, been involved in the murder of her Tory employer, an act of grave insubordination—but the Reform newspapers that praised Mackenzie were also inclined to clemency towards Grace. This split in opinion continued through later writers on the case right up to the end of the nineteenth century.

I felt that, to be fair, I had to represent all points of view. I devised the following set of guidelines for myself: when there was a solid fact, I could not alter it; long as I might to have Grace witness McDermott's execution, it could not be done, because, worse luck, she was already in the Penitentiary on that day. Also, every major element in the book had to be suggested by something in the writing about Grace and her times, however dubious such writing might be; but in the parts left unexplained—the gaps left unfilled—I was free to invent. Since there were a lot of gaps, there is a lot of invention. *Alias Grace* is very much a novel rather than a documentary.

As I wrote, I found myself considering the number and variety of the stories that had been told: Grace's own versions—there were several—as reported in the newspapers and in her "Confession"; McDermott's versions, also multiple; Moodie's version; and those of the later commentators. For each story, there was a teller, but—as is true of all stories—there was also an audience; both were influenced by received climates of opinion about politics, and also about criminality and its proper treatment, about the nature of women—their weakness and seductive qualities, for instance—and about insanity, in fact, about everything that had a bearing on the case.

In my fiction, Grace too—whatever else she is—is a storyteller, with strong motives to narrate, but also strong motives to withhold; the only power left to her as a convicted and imprisoned criminal comes from a blend of these two motives. What is told by her to her audience of one, Dr. Simon Jordan—who is not only a more educated person than she is, but a man, which gave him an automatic edge in the nineteenth century, and a man with the potential to be of help to her—is selective, of course. It is dependent on what she remembers; or is it what she says she remembers, which can be quite a different thing? And how can her audience tell the difference? Here we are, right back at the end of the twentieth century, with our own uneasiness about the trustworthiness of memory, the reliability of story, and the continuity of time. As I have said, we cannot help but be contemporary, and *Alias Grace*, although set in the mid-nineteenth century, is, of course, a very contemporary book. In a Victorian novel, Grace would say, "Now it all comes back to me." But as *Alias Grace* is not a Victorian novel, she does not say that, and if she did, would we—any longer—believe her?

These are the sorts of questions that my own fictional excursions into the nevertheless real Canadian past left me asking. Nor did it escape me that a different writer, with access to exactly the same historical records, could have—and without doubt would have—written a very different sort of novel. I am not one of those who believes there is no truth to be known. But I have to conclude that, although there undoubtedly was a truth—somebody did kill Nancy Montgomery—truth is sometimes unknowable, at least by us.

What does the past tell us? In and of itself, it tells us nothing. We have to be listening first, before it will say a word; and even so, listening means telling, and then re-telling. It's we ourselves who must do such telling, about the past, if anything is to be said about it; and our audience is one another. After we in our turn have become the past, others will tell stories about us, and about our times; or will not, as the case may be. Unlikely as it seems, it is possible that we may not interest them. Worse, they may not exist.

But meanwhile, while we still have the chance, what should we ourselves tell? Or rather, what *do* we tell? Individual memory, history, and the novel are all selective: no one remembers everything, each historian picks out the facts he or she chooses to find significant, and every novel, whether historical or not, must limit its own scope. No one can tell all the stories there are. As for novelists, it's best if they confine themselves to the Ancient Mariner stories, that is, the stories that seize hold of them and torment them until they have grabbed a batch of unsuspecting Wedding Guests with their skinny hands, and held them with their glittering eyes or else their glittering prose, and told them a tale they cannot choose but hear.

Such stories are not about this or that slice of the past, or this or that political or social event, or this or that city or country or nationality, although, of course, these may enter into it, and often do. They are about human nature, which usually means they are about pride, envy, avarice, lust, sloth, gluttony, and anger. They are about truth and lies, and disguises and revelations; they are about crime and punishment; they are about love and forgiveness and long-suffering and charity, they are about sin and retribution and sometimes even redemption.

In the recent film *Il Postino*, the great poet Pablo Neruda upbraids his friend, a lowly postman, for having filched one of Neruda's poems to use in his courtship of a local girl. "But," replies the postman, "poems do not belong to those who write them. Poems belong to those who need them." And so it is with stories about the past. The past no longer belongs only to those who lived in it; the past belongs to those who claim it, and are willing to explore it, and to infuse it with meaning for those alive today. The past belongs to us, because we are the ones who need it.

Printed in October 1997 by
VEILLEUX
ON DEMAND PRINTING INC.
in Boucherville, Quebec